ROCKS

Chris Oxlade

Edited by Helen Cox Cannons
Designed by Philippa Jenkins
Illustrated by sprout.uk.com p. 4, p. 11; International Mapping p. 13; HL Studios p. 23
Original illustrations © Capstone Global Library Limited 2016
Picture research by Tracy Cummins
Production by Victoria Fitzgerald
Originated by Capstone Global Library Limited
Printed and bound in China

19 18 17 16 15
10 9 8 7 6 5 4 3 2 1

Library of Congress Cataloging-in-Publication Data
Cataloging-in-publication information is on file with the Library of Congress.
ISBN 978-1-4109-8135-6 (library binding)
ISBN 978-1-4109-8143-1 (eBook PDF)

Acknowledgments
The author and publisher are grateful to the following for permission to reproduce copyright material:
Capstone Press: HL Studios, 23, International Mapping, 13, Karon Dubke, 28, 29, sprout.uk.com, 4 Top, 11; Corbis: LUCAS JACKSON/Reuters, 24; Getty Images: Carsten Peter, 21, Education Images/UIG, 20; Science Source: Joel Arem, 18; Shutterstock: botazsolti, 26, Bragin Alexey, 8, claffra, 22, dexns, 14, Erik Harrison, 17, fivespots, 19, Francesco R. Iacomino, 4 Bottom, Jakub Houdek, 7, Jay Boucher, 6, jordache, 27, LianeM, 10, MarcelClemens, 12, orangecrush, 25, Radoslaw Lecyk, Cover, 1; Thinkstock: Elena Elisseeva, 9, Sam Camp, 15, takepicsforfun, 16.

The author would like to thank Dr. Gillian Fyfe for her invaluable help in the preparation of this book.

Every effort has been made to contact copyright holders of any material reproduced in this book. Any omissions will be rectified in subsequent printings if notice is given to the publisher.

All the Internet addresses (URLs) given in this book were valid at the time of going to press. However, due to the dynamic nature of the Internet, some addresses may have changed, or sites may have changed or ceased to exist since publication. While the author and publisher regret any inconvenience this may cause readers, no responsibility for any such changes can be accepted by either the author or the publisher.

What Are Rocks?..4

Where Do We Find Rocks? 6

What Are Rocks Made From? 8

What Are Igneous Rocks? 10

What Are Sedimentary Rocks?............................14

What Are Metamorphic Rocks? 18

How Do Rocks Change over Time? 20

What Do We Use Rocks For?................................24

Identify Rocks That You Find 28

Glossary... 30

Find Out More...31

Index 32

Some words are shown in bold, **like this**. You can find out what they mean by looking in the glossary.

Rocks are natural, nonliving materials. They are part of our planet, Earth. Rocks make up the part of Earth called the **crust**. The crust is a hard outer layer, like the crust on a loaf of bread. All the rocky features we see on Earth's surface, such as mountains, seaside cliffs, and caves, are part of the crust.

The science of rocks is called geology. The scientists who study geology are called **geologists.**

core

outer core

mantle

upper mantle

This diagram shows the layers of rock inside Earth.

This sandstone rock in Arizona shows layers of rock very clearly.

Three Types of Rock

There are three main types of rock: **igneous rocks,** **sedimentary rocks,** and **metamorphic rocks.**

- *Igneous rocks* are made when molten (melted) rock cools and hardens.
- *Sedimentary rocks* are formed from layers of **sediment**. This sediment is made up of mud, sand, or shells.
- *Metamorphic rocks* are made when other rocks are heated up or squeezed by huge forces.

Useful Rocks

Rocks are useful materials. The rock we use is known as stone. You might live in a building that is either built from or decorated with stone. Walls of old buildings might be made from stone. You might have ornaments or jewelry made from stone. Stone was one of the first materials that our distant ancestors used.

ROCK SOLID FACTS!

THE OLDEST ROCKS

Earth is 4.6 billion years old. Most of the rocks on Earth's surface are much younger than that, but geologists have found igneous rocks that are 4.5 billion years old in Australia. They are the oldest rocks discovered on Earth.

Wherever you are in the world, there will be rocks not far under your feet. In most places, we cannot see the rocks. That is because the rocks are hidden underneath soil, forests, plants, ice, and snow. Rocks are also underneath human-made objects such as roads, sidewalks, buildings, and yards. Oceans and seas cover two-thirds of Earth's surface, but there is rock under the seabed, too.

These high cliffs are in Yosemite National Park in California.

Where to See Rocks

Mountains are the best places to see rocks, because there is no soil on steep mountainsides to cover up the rocks. The rocks make up jagged peaks, steep cliff faces, and scree slopes. Scree slopes are steep slopes made of stones and boulders.

ROCKS IN SPACE

There are lumps of rock drifting around in space. Sometimes these lumps collide with (bump into) Earth. Most of them burn up as they burst into Earth's **atmosphere**. But some lumps get through and hit Earth's surface, and these are called meteorites.

The Hoba meteorite in Namibia, Africa, is the largest meteorite ever found. ⟹

Rocks are also easy to spot in canyons, where rivers have cut deep into layers of rock. You can also see them in deserts, where the wind blows away sand, on the coast, where the sea wears away the coast, and in quarries.

Local Rocks

If you don't live near mountains or on the coast, you can still see rocks every day. The soil in your yard or a park contains tiny pieces of rock and stones. Many buildings are built with stone or decorated with tiles that contain stone. Roads are made with **gravel**. Some ornaments are made from stone, too. Why not see how much rock you can find around your home?

All rocks are made from materials called **minerals**. Minerals are natural, nonliving materials from Earth's **crust**. Most rocks are made from two, three, or more different minerals mixed together. **Geologists** have found more than 4,000 different minerals in Earth's crust.

Examples of Minerals

Some minerals are much more common than others. Two minerals called feldspar and quartz are easily the most common minerals. Feldspar makes up more than half of Earth's crust. Halite is another common mineral. We see halite fairly often because the salt that we put on food is halite.

There are pieces of quartz and feldspar in this chunk of granite. ⇒

MINERALS AS CRYSTALS

Geodes are empty spaces inside rocks. The geodes are often lined with beautiful crystals. The crystals are made of minerals that grew inside the geode over millions of years.

Mineral Pieces

Different minerals come in different colors and shine in different ways. This means it is often easy to see the different minerals in a piece of rock. You can easily see the different minerals in the photograph of a piece of granite on page 8. But in many rocks, the pieces of different minerals are too small to see without a microscope.

The Makeup of Rocks

Some **sedimentary rocks** are made up of bits and pieces of rock, such as mud, **silt**, sand, **gravel**, and pebbles. Other sedimentary rocks, such as chalk and limestone, are made up of the shells and skeletons of animals and other creatures that lived in the sea long ago.

As we learned on page 5, **igneous rocks** are rocks made when molten (melted) rock cools down and turns to solid rock. You can imagine how this happens by thinking about hot, molten wax running down the side of a candle. When the wax cools down at the base of the candle, it turns back into a solid. The same thing happens when igneous rocks are formed. The word "igneous" means fire.

Molten Magma

Deep underneath Earth's **crust**, there is rock that is incredibly hot and slightly soft. Sometimes this hot rock melts to make molten rock, which is called **magma**. Magma pushes its way upward through cracks in Earth's crust and rises toward the surface.

Igneous rock called basalt sometimes splits up into columns, like this.

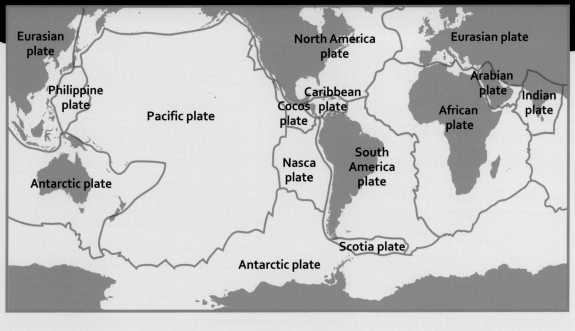

This map shows all of the world's tectonic plates.

Crusty Plates

Earth's crust is cracked into giant pieces, which are called tectonic plates. The cracks where the edge of one plate meets the edge of another are called plate boundaries. At some boundaries the edges of the plates are moving apart, and at other boundaries the edges are crushed together. Magma often pushes up through the crust along these plate boundaries. Magma also rises at places called hot spots. These are weak parts of the crust not close to plate boundaries.

Hawaiian Hot Spots

The islands of Hawaii are the tops of giant volcanoes that have grown over a hot spot in Earth's crust. Kilauea volcano on Hawaii is one of the world's most active volcanoes. New igneous rock is being made here nearly all the time.

Volcanic Rocks

Sometimes **magma** that pushes up into Earth's **crust** reaches all the way to the surface and comes out of the ground. It cools and forms new rock. A place where magma comes out of the ground is called a volcano. Or, if it is a long crack in the surface, it's called a fissure. **Igneous rocks** formed on the surface of Earth are called volcanic rocks.

When this runny magma reaches the surface of the volcano, it is called **lava**. It forms red-hot rivers called lava flows. The lava slowly cools in the air. Eventually it stops flowing and turns to solid rock.

At other volcanoes, thick, gooey magma blasts into the air. This makes clouds of volcanic ash. The ash falls from the air and builds up to make layers of volcanic rock.

This lava in Hawaii is cooling and turning to solid rock.

ROCK SOLID FACTS!

GIANT ERUPTION

About 60 million years ago, there were giant eruptions of lava in the part of the world that is now in the west of India. The eruptions continued on and off for hundreds of thousands of years. The lava made a layer of igneous rock more than 6,600 feet (2,000 meters) thick. This area is known as the Deccan Traps.

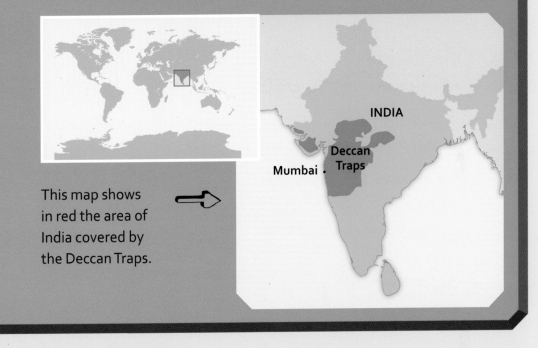

This map shows in red the area of India covered by the Deccan Traps.

Rocks Under the Sea

Many volcanoes erupt under the sea. The lava cools very quickly in cold seawater, making humps and lumps of new rock called pillow lava.

Underground Rocks

Often magma does not reach the surface. Sometimes magma fills cracks in the rock around it, but it can also fill huge underground domes. It cools very slowly under the ground and turns to new rock.

As we learned on page 5, **sedimentary rocks** are made from layers of mud, **silt**, sand, **gravel**, and pebbles. They also contain the shells or skeletons of animals that once lived in the sea. These layers are called **sediments**. If you have been to a beach before, then you have seen sediments—the sand on a beach is an example of sediment.

Rocky Particles

Some sedimentary rocks are made up of pieces of rock stuck together. For example, sandstone is made from grains of sand. You can see and feel the grains if you pick up a piece of sandstone.

This shows sedimentary rock layers.

Sources of Sediment

The pieces of rock in sedimentary rocks are made when other rocks get broken up. These rocks could be **igneous rocks**, **metamorphic rocks**, or other sedimentary rocks. The weather, flowing water, and breaking waves can smash up the rocks into small pieces. You can find out how this happens on pages 20–21.

Dropping Sediments

Tiny specks of rock (seen only through a microscope) are carried down rivers, washed along in the sea, or blown by the wind. Later, they are dropped in rivers, on beaches, or on the seabed. All these tiny specks cause layers of sediment to be made. If sediment gets buried deeper under more sediment, the rocky pieces get crushed and squeezed down to form rock. It can take millions of years for the loose sediment to turn to solid rock.

This river has dropped sediment at the point where it becomes sea.

Rocks from Animals

Some **sedimentary rocks**, including chalk and some limestones, are made from millions of shells, skeletons, and other hard parts of tiny creatures that live in the sea. The shells and other parts slowly build up into layers of muddy **sediment**. As more layers are added, the layers underneath slowly turn to rock.

Fossils in Sedimentary Rocks

Fossils form when animals or plants die. Their remains are trapped in the sediments that become sedimentary rocks later. The hard parts of the animals' bodies, such as their bones and teeth, are turned to rock.

Rocks from Water

Have you ever watched salty water dry up, leaving dry white salt behind? Some rocks form like this. They are called evaporite rocks. This is because the water has evaporated (dried up). Stalactites and stalagmites in caves are made of an evaporite rock called calcite.

These evaporite rocks are a type of limestone called travertine.

ROCK SOLID FACTS!

GRAND CANYON FOSSILS

The mighty cliffs of the Grand Canyon in Arizona are made from sedimentary rocks. The Colorado River has slowly cut down through many different layers of rock to create a giant canyon. We can see the layers in the canyon's cliffs.

A layer of rock near the top of the canyon was formed on the bottom of an ocean 250 million years ago. It is 330 feet (100 meters) deep and contains many fossils of sea creatures. The rocks at the canyon's bottom were made more than 1 billion years ago.

As we learned on page 5, **metamorphic rocks** are made when rocks are changed. The word "metamorphic" comes from the word "metamorphosis." It means that something changes from one form to another (such as when a caterpillar turns into a butterfly).

The original rocks that get turned into metamorphic rocks can be **igneous rocks, sedimentary rocks,** or other metamorphic rocks. For example, slate is a metamorphic rock made from a sedimentary rock called shale.

Heat and Pressure

Rocks change into metamorphic rocks when they are heated up and squeezed by pressure on them. It takes a massive amount of heat and pressure to make metamorphic rocks. These conditions are only found deep in Earth's **crust** and around volcanoes. The heat and pressure on the rocks turn the **minerals** inside them into different minerals. This rearranges the layers of rock.

This is a metamorphic rock called schist.

SPECTACULAR STONES

Precious gemstones such as emeralds, rubies, and sapphires are all found in metamorphic rocks. They form when the heat and pressure deep in Earth's crust are creating metamorphic rocks.

Tanzanite (blue zoisite) is a rare gemstone found only in the Merelani Hills in Tanzania. Tanzanite was formed millions of years ago from metamorphic rock.

Rocks Under Mountains

Many metamorphic rocks are made where the **tectonic plates** that make up Earth's crust push against each other (see page 11). Massive forces squeeze the rocks at the edges of the plates. This happens on a grand scale, where huge mountain ranges are pushed up at the same time. For example, there are metamorphic rocks found under the Himalaya mountain range in Asia.

The rocks under our feet seem solid, but in fact they are changing all the time. We have already seen how new **igneous rocks**, **sedimentary rocks**, and **metamorphic rocks** are made. While this is happening, older rocks are destroyed. We do not normally notice these changes, because they mostly happen very, very slowly.

Breaking Up Rocks

The rocks on Earth's surface are slowly worn away. There are two processes that wear them away, called weathering and **erosion**.

The rocks are eroded by glaciers as they flow downhill.

DISSOLVING ROCKS

Caves are made when streams flow underground through limestone rocks. The limestone slowly dissolves in the water. This process created the biggest cave in the world, the Son Doong Cave in Vietnam. It is 5.6 miles (9 kilometers) long and is so big that it has its own river and jungle!

Weathering

Weathering is caused by weather conditions. Imagine a rock in a desert. During the day the Sun heats up the rock, but in the cold night the rock cools again. This makes the rock expand and shrink, which makes it crumble. Now imagine a rock on a mountain. Rainwater seeps into a crack in the rock, then freezes at night. The ice pushes sideways, making the crack wider. Eventually, the rock splits in two.

Erosion

Erosion is caused by flowing water, waves, wind, and ice. Flowing water breaks up rocks and carries the broken pieces away. Crashing waves break up rocks on shores. Strong winds pick up tiny specks of rock and carry them along. **Glaciers** scrape away rocks as they flow slowly downhill from mountains.

21

These layers of rock at Lulworth Cove, in England, have been folded by massive forces.

Melting and Bending

In addition to being changed by weathering and **erosion**, rocks are changed under the ground by very high temperatures and huge forces.

Some rocks are destroyed at the boundaries between Earth's **tectonic plates** (see page 11). This happens where two plates collide. The edge of one plate slides underneath the edge of the other plate. When this happens, the edge of the lower plate gets pushed many miles down. It slides into super-hot layers of rock under the **crust** and melts. As a result, the rocks that make up the plate are destroyed.

Where tectonic plates collide with each other, rocks can also be scrunched up by huge forces. The crushed rock sometimes forms whole new mountain ranges. We can see bent layers of **sedimentary rocks** in seaside cliffs.

New Rocks

New **igneous** and sedimentary rocks are being made all the time. New igneous rocks are made every time a volcano erupts and when **magma** cools under the ground. New sedimentary rocks are made from bits and pieces of rock, shells, and skeletons under the oceans.

The Rock Cycle

New rocks are being made all the time while old rocks are being changed or destroyed. These changes are known as the rock cycle. The cycle has been working since Earth was made billions of years ago. It is working now and will keep working for billions more years.

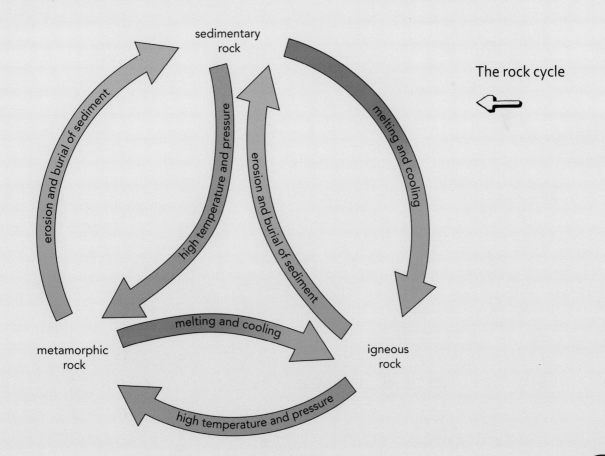

The rock cycle

Rocks are really useful materials. We use rocks in more places than you might think—from delicate jewelry to giant sea defenses.

Rocks for Building

Builders and engineers use stone for many different jobs. Many rocks are very hard materials, so they are difficult to crush. This makes them good for building walls in houses and gardens. The strong rocks at the bottom of a wall hold up the heavy stones above.

Heavy lumps of rock protect the coast against waves.

STONE TOOLS

Tens of thousands of years ago, wood, bone, shells, and stone were the only materials that people could find. Early humans made axes and arrowheads by chipping at a rock called flint. Flint breaks naturally into pieces with sharp edges.

The 15th-century Inca city of Machu Picchu is built of closely fitting stones.

Building bricks are shaped from clay, then heated in a kiln. This makes the clay turn very hard. Slate is a **metamorphic rock** that splits easily into thin layers. So, slate is a good material for making roof tiles and floor tiles. **Gravel** (small pebbles) and sand are used in making concrete.

Rock for Decoration

Many rocks and **minerals** show beautiful colors and patterns when they are cut and polished. They are perfect for use in decoration. For example, rocks such as marble and granite are sawed into sheets to make floor tiles, wall tiles, and countertops. Sculptors use these rocks for carving statues or other objects, too.

Using Minerals

We know that all rocks are made of **minerals**. Precious stones such as diamonds and sapphires are minerals found in rocks. We use them in jewelry because of their color and sparkle. Precious stones are also used in industry (manufacturing). For example, small, unpolished diamonds are glued onto drill bits because diamonds are harder than metal.

Many minerals are useful in farming. Limestone is made mostly of a mineral called calcite. Spreading calcite on fields makes the soil better for growing crops. Calcite is also used in cement and paints.

Metals from Rocks

All metals come from minerals in rocks. The minerals we get metals from are called **ores**. We make all sorts of objects, from tiny screws to giant spacecraft, from the metals in minerals. For example, iron is part of a mineral ore called hematite.

The drill bit on a dental drill is coated with powdered diamonds.

Iron is released from iron ore in an iron smelter like this one. ⟹

Metals from Minerals

To get metals out of minerals, we heat the minerals to make them melt. We then collect the metal that runs out. Gold is found in sheets covering other rocks or in lumps called nuggets, which are found in **gravel**.

ROCK SOLID FACTS!

HEAT FROM ROCKS

In areas of the world where there are volcanoes, the rocks underground are very hot. We can collect this heat and use it to warm our homes. To collect it, water is pumped down into the ground. When the water comes back to the surface, it is boiling hot.

Identify Rocks That You Find

If you find interesting rocks while you are outside, it's fun to try to identify what kinds of rocks they are. There are hundreds of different types of rock. Try to figure out whether a rock is an **igneous rock**, a **sedimentary rock**, or a **metamorphic rock**.

What you need:

- some pieces or rock
- a small magnifying glass (called a hand lens)

❶ Start by looking at the piece of rock with your naked eye, and then with a magnifying glass. Also feel the texture of the rock.

❷ If you can see rounded or jagged bits and pieces of rock of different sizes and you can feel grains of rock, like sand, then:
- the rock is almost certainly a sedimentary rock, such as breccia or sandstone.

❸ If you can see fossils in the rock, then:
  • it also a sedimentary rock.

❹ If you can see shells in the rock, then:
  • it is a limestone.

❺ If you can see bands of color through the rock, possibly in wavy lines, then:
  • it is probably a metamorphic rock, such as schist or gneiss.

❻ If you can see the rock is made up of crystals of different-colored **minerals**, then:
  • it is probably an igneous rock, such as granite or gabbro.

❼ If you think you have identified a piece of rock, label it. Try making a collection of different rock samples.

Glossary

atmosphere layer of air that surrounds Earth

crust thin layer of hard rock that makes up the surface of Earth

erosion gradual wearing away of something

geologist scientist who studies rocks and minerals

glacier slow-moving river of ice that flows down from a mountain range

gravel loose material made up of small pieces of rock (the pieces can be as small as peas or as large as grapes)

igneous rock rock made when molten rock cools and hardens

lava molten, or hot liquid, rock that is on the surface of Earth

magma molten, or hot liquid, rock that is underground

metamorphic rock rock made when other rocks are heated up or squeezed by immense forces

mineral natural, nonliving materials found in Earth's crust

ore rock that we get metals or other minerals from

sediment tiny specks of rock, seen only through a microscope, that build up to make layers of sand, mud, or silt

sedimentary rock rock made from layers of sediment

silt sediment with tiny pieces in it, smaller than in sand but larger than in clay

tectonic plate one of the giant pieces that Earth's crust has been cracked into

Books

Oxlade, Chris. *Rocks and Minerals.* Essential Physical Science. Chicago: Heinemann Library, 2014.

Spilsbury, Louise. *What Is the Rock Cycle?* Let's Find Out! New York: Britannica/Rosen, 2014.

Weidner Zoehfeld, Kathy. *Rocks and Minerals.* National Geographic Readers. Washington, D.C.: National Geographic, 2012.

Internet Sites

www.geography4kids.com/files/earth_rocktypes.html
Learn more about the different types of rock here.

www.kidsloverocks.com
This fun website will teach you all about rocks and also help you learn how to start your own rock collection.

www.learner.org/interactives/rockcycle/index.html
This website has activities and shows you different rocks and how to identify them.

canyons, 7, 17
caves, 4, 16, 21
cliffs, 4, 6, 17, 22
coasts, 7, 24
colors, 9, 25, 26

erosion, 20–21, 22
evaporite rocks, 16

feldspar, 8
fossils, 16–17

gemstones, 19, 26
geodes, 9
geologists, 4–5, 8
geology, 4
Grand Canyon 17
gravel 7, 9, 14, 27

igneous rocks, 5, 10–11, 12–13, 15, 18, 20, 23

magma, 10–11, 12–13, 23
metamorphic rocks, 5, 15, 18–19, 20, 25
minerals, 8–9, 18, 25, 26–27
mountains, 4, 6–7, 19, 21, 22

ores 26, 27

pebbles 9, 14, 25

quarries, 7
quartz, 8

sand 5, 7, 9, 14, 25, 28
sandstone 4, 14, 28
sedimentary rocks, 5, 9, 14–15, 16–17, 18, 20, 22–23
sediment 5, 15
stone 5, 6, 7, 24, 25

tectonic plates, 11, 19, 22

volcanoes, 11, 12–13, 18, 23, 2

weathering, 20–21, 22

uses of rocks, 24–25, 26–27